This book was made to manage your budget for the year. The first of page of the month is to set goals and priorities, tasks and things you set out to do and don't want to miss. The second one is for the monthly overall plan. The next four pages is to address the weekly. Then the next page is for your notes, like other information or training you don't want to miss, and lastly this page is to jot down overall ideas. Don't have all the fun by yourself. Get some friends, siblings, students to join you and do it together. Prosperity is your birthright and let no on tell you otherwise.

January

Notes

Priority

1.
2.
3.
4.
5.

Tasks

- [ ]
- [ ]
- [ ]
- [ ]

Don't Forget

MONTHLY BUDGET

MONTH: ______________________ BUDGET GOAL: ______________

YOUR INCOME			
DATE	SOURCE	GROSS AMOUNT	NET AFTER TAX

FIXED EXPENSES		
DATE	DESCRIPTION	AMOUNT
	TOTAL	

VARIABLES EXPENSES		
DATE	DESCRIPTION	AMOUNT
	TOTAL	

	MONTHLY TOTALS		
	BUDGTED	ACTUAL	DIFFERENCE
TOTAL INCOME			
TOTAL EXPENSES			
TOTAL SAVINGS			

EXPENSE TRACKER

MONTH: ______________________________

DATE	DESCRIPTION	CATEGORY	NET AFTER TAX
		TOTAL	

EXPENSE TRACKER

MONTH: ______________________________

DATE	DESCRIPTION	CATEGORY	NET AFTER TAX
		TOTAL	

EXPENSE TRACKER

MONTH: ______________________

DATE	DESCRIPTION	CATEGORY	NET AFTER TAX
		TOTAL	

EXPENSE TRACKER

MONTH: ______________________________

DATE	DESCRIPTION	CATEGORY	NET AFTER TAX
		TOTAL	

NOTES

Brain Bump

February

Notes

Priority

1.
2.
3.
4.
5.

Tasks

- [ ]
- [ ]
- [ ]
- [ ]

Don't Forget

MONTHLY BUDGET

MONTH: ______________________ BUDGET GOAL: ____________

YOUR INCOME			
DATE	SOURCE	GROSS AMOUNT	NET AFTER TAX

FIXED EXPENSES		
DATE	DESCRIPTION	AMOUNT
	TOTAL	

VARIABLES EXPENSES		
DATE	DESCRIPTION	AMOUNT
	TOTAL	

	MONTHLY TOTALS		
	BUDGTED	ACTUAL	DIFFERENCE
TOTAL INCOME			
TOTAL EXPENSES			
TOTAL SAVINGS			

EXPENSE TRACKER

MONTH: ______________________________

DATE	DESCRIPTION	CATEGORY	NET AFTER TAX
		TOTAL	

EXPENSE TRACKER

MONTH: ______________________________

DATE	DESCRIPTION	CATEGORY	NET AFTER TAX
		TOTAL	

EXPENSE TRACKER

MONTH: ______________________

DATE	DESCRIPTION	CATEGORY	NET AFTER TAX
		TOTAL	

EXPENSE TRACKER

MONTH: ____________________

DATE	DESCRIPTION	CATEGORY	NET AFTER TAX
		TOTAL	

NOTES

Brain Bump

March

Notes

Priority

1.
2.
3.
4.
5.

Tasks

- [ ]
- [ ]
- [ ]
- [ ]

Don't Forget

MONTHLY BUDGET

MONTH: ____________________ BUDGET GOAL: ____________

YOUR INCOME			
DATE	SOURCE	GROSS AMOUNT	NET AFTER TAX

FIXED EXPENSES		
DATE	DESCRIPTION	AMOUNT
	TOTAL	

VARIABLES EXPENSES		
DATE	DESCRIPTION	AMOUNT
	TOTAL	

	MONTHLY TOTALS		
	BUDGTED	ACTUAL	DIFFERENCE
TOTAL INCOME			
TOTAL EXPENSES			
TOTAL SAVINGS			

EXPENSE TRACKER

MONTH: ______________________________

DATE	DESCRIPTION	CATEGORY	NET AFTER TAX
		TOTAL	

EXPENSE TRACKER

MONTH: ______________________________

DATE	DESCRIPTION	CATEGORY	NET AFTER TAX
		TOTAL	

EXPENSE TRACKER

MONTH: ____________________

DATE	DESCRIPTION	CATEGORY	NET AFTER TAX
		TOTAL	

EXPENSE TRACKER

MONTH: ______________________________

DATE	DESCRIPTION	CATEGORY	NET AFTER TAX
		TOTAL	

NOTES

Brain Bump

April

Notes

Priority

1.
2.
3.
4.
5.

Tasks

- [ ]
- [ ]
- [ ]
- [ ]

Don't Forget

MONTHLY BUDGET

MONTH: ______________________ BUDGET GOAL: ____________

YOUR INCOME			
DATE	SOURCE	GROSS AMOUNT	NET AFTER TAX

FIXED EXPENSES		
DATE	DESCRIPTION	AMOUNT
	TOTAL	

VARIABLES EXPENSES		
DATE	DESCRIPTION	AMOUNT
	TOTAL	

	MONTHLY TOTALS		
	BUDGTED	ACTUAL	DIFFERENCE
TOTAL INCOME			
TOTAL EXPENSES			
TOTAL SAVINGS			

EXPENSE TRACKER

MONTH: ______________________________

DATE	DESCRIPTION	CATEGORY	NET AFTER TAX
			TOTAL	

EXPENSE TRACKER

MONTH: ____________________

DATE	DESCRIPTION	CATEGORY	NET AFTER TAX
		TOTAL	

EXPENSE TRACKER

MONTH: ______________________________

DATE	DESCRIPTION	CATEGORY	NET AFTER TAX
		TOTAL	

EXPENSE TRACKER

MONTH: ______________________________

DATE	DESCRIPTION	CATEGORY	NET AFTER TAX
		TOTAL	

NOTES

Brain Bump

May

Notes

Priority

1.
2.
3.
4.
5.

Tasks

- [ ]
- [ ]
- [ ]
- [ ]

Don't Forget

MONTHLY BUDGET

MONTH: ____________________ BUDGET GOAL: ____________

YOUR INCOME			
DATE	SOURCE	GROSS AMOUNT	NET AFTER TAX

FIXED EXPENSES		
DATE	DESCRIPTION	AMOUNT
	TOTAL	

VARIABLES EXPENSES		
DATE	DESCRIPTION	AMOUNT
	TOTAL	

	MONTHLY TOTALS		
	BUDGTED	ACTUAL	DIFFERENCE
TOTAL INCOME			
TOTAL EXPENSES			
TOTAL SAVINGS			

EXPENSE TRACKER

MONTH: ______________________

DATE	DESCRIPTION	CATEGORY	NET AFTER TAX
		TOTAL	

EXPENSE TRACKER

MONTH: ______________________________

DATE	DESCRIPTION	CATEGORY	NET AFTER TAX
		TOTAL	

EXPENSE TRACKER

MONTH: ____________________

DATE	DESCRIPTION	CATEGORY	NET AFTER TAX
		TOTAL	

EXPENSE TRACKER

MONTH: ______________________

DATE	DESCRIPTION	CATEGORY	NET AFTER TAX
		TOTAL	

NOTES

Brain Bump

June

Notes

Priority

1.
2.
3.
4.
5.

Tasks

- [ ]
- [ ]
- [ ]
- [ ]

Don't Forget

MONTHLY BUDGET

MONTH: ______________________ BUDGET GOAL: ____________

YOUR INCOME			
DATE	SOURCE	GROSS AMOUNT	NET AFTER TAX

FIXED EXPENSES		
DATE	DESCRIPTION	AMOUNT
	TOTAL	

VARIABLES EXPENSES		
DATE	DESCRIPTION	AMOUNT
	TOTAL	

	MONTHLY TOTALS		
	BUDGTED	ACTUAL	DIFFERENCE
TOTAL INCOME			
TOTAL EXPENSES			
TOTAL SAVINGS			

EXPENSE TRACKER

MONTH: ______________________________

DATE	DESCRIPTION	CATEGORY	NET AFTER TAX
		TOTAL	

EXPENSE TRACKER

MONTH: ____________________________

DATE	DESCRIPTION	CATEGORY	NET AFTER TAX
		TOTAL	

EXPENSE TRACKER

MONTH: ______________________

DATE	DESCRIPTION	CATEGORY	NET AFTER TAX
		TOTAL	

EXPENSE TRACKER

MONTH: ______________________________

DATE	DESCRIPTION	CATEGORY	NET AFTER TAX
		TOTAL	

NOTES

Brain Bump

July

Notes

Priority

1.
2.
3.
4.
5.

Tasks

- [ ]
- [ ]
- [ ]
- [ ]

Don't Forget

MONTHLY BUDGET

MONTH: ____________________ BUDGET GOAL: ______________

YOUR INCOME			
DATE	SOURCE	GROSS AMOUNT	NET AFTER TAX

FIXED EXPENSES		
DATE	DESCRIPTION	AMOUNT
	TOTAL	

VARIABLES EXPENSES		
DATE	DESCRIPTION	AMOUNT
	TOTAL	

	MONTHLY TOTALS		
	BUDGTED	ACTUAL	DIFFERENCE
TOTAL INCOME			
TOTAL EXPENSES			
TOTAL SAVINGS			

EXPENSE TRACKER

MONTH: ______________________

DATE	DESCRIPTION	CATEGORY	NET AFTER TAX
		TOTAL	

EXPENSE TRACKER

MONTH: ______________________

DATE	DESCRIPTION	CATEGORY	NET AFTER TAX
		TOTAL	

EXPENSE TRACKER

MONTH: ____________________

DATE	DESCRIPTION	CATEGORY	NET AFTER TAX
		TOTAL	

EXPENSE TRACKER

MONTH: ______________________________

DATE	DESCRIPTION	CATEGORY	NET AFTER TAX
		TOTAL	

NOTES

Brain Bump

August

Notes

Priority

1.
2.
3.
4.
5.

Tasks

- [ ]
- [ ]
- [ ]
- [ ]

Don't Forget

MONTHLY BUDGET

MONTH: ______________________ BUDGET GOAL: ______________

YOUR INCOME			
DATE	SOURCE	GROSS AMOUNT	NET AFTER TAX

FIXED EXPENSES		
DATE	DESCRIPTION	AMOUNT
	TOTAL	

VARIABLES EXPENSES		
DATE	DESCRIPTION	AMOUNT
	TOTAL	

	MONTHLY TOTALS		
	BUDGTED	ACTUAL	DIFFERENCE
TOTAL INCOME			
TOTAL EXPENSES			
TOTAL SAVINGS			

EXPENSE TRACKER

MONTH: ______________________________

DATE	DESCRIPTION	CATEGORY	NET AFTER TAX
		TOTAL	

EXPENSE TRACKER

MONTH: ______________________________

DATE	DESCRIPTION	CATEGORY	NET AFTER TAX
		TOTAL	

EXPENSE TRACKER

MONTH: ______________________________

DATE	DESCRIPTION	CATEGORY	NET AFTER TAX
		TOTAL	

EXPENSE TRACKER

MONTH: ______________________

DATE	DESCRIPTION	CATEGORY	NET AFTER TAX
		TOTAL	

NOTES

Brain Bump

September

Notes

Priority

1. __________
2. __________
3. __________
4. __________
5. __________

Tasks

- [ ] __________
- [ ] __________
- [ ] __________
- [ ] __________

Don't Forget

MONTHLY BUDGET

MONTH: ____________________ BUDGET GOAL: ____________

YOUR INCOME			
DATE	SOURCE	GROSS AMOUNT	NET AFTER TAX

FIXED EXPENSES		
DATE	DESCRIPTION	AMOUNT
	TOTAL	

VARIABLES EXPENSES		
DATE	DESCRIPTION	AMOUNT
	TOTAL	

	MONTHLY TOTALS		
	BUDGTED	ACTUAL	DIFFERENCE
TOTAL INCOME			
TOTAL EXPENSES			
TOTAL SAVINGS			

EXPENSE TRACKER

MONTH: ______________________________

DATE	DESCRIPTION	CATEGORY	NET AFTER TAX
		TOTAL	

EXPENSE TRACKER

MONTH: ______________________________

DATE	DESCRIPTION	CATEGORY	NET AFTER TAX
		TOTAL	

EXPENSE TRACKER

MONTH: ______________________________

DATE	DESCRIPTION	CATEGORY	NET AFTER TAX
		TOTAL	

EXPENSE TRACKER

MONTH: ____________________

DATE	DESCRIPTION	CATEGORY	NET AFTER TAX
		TOTAL	

NOTES

Brain Bump

October

Notes

Priority

1.
2.
3.
4.
5.

Tasks

- [ ]
- [ ]
- [ ]
- [ ]

Don't Forget

MONTHLY BUDGET

MONTH: ______________________ BUDGET GOAL: ____________

YOUR INCOME			
DATE	SOURCE	GROSS AMOUNT	NET AFTER TAX

FIXED EXPENSES		
DATE	DESCRIPTION	AMOUNT
	TOTAL	

VARIABLES EXPENSES		
DATE	DESCRIPTION	AMOUNT
	TOTAL	

	MONTHLY TOTALS		
	BUDGTED	ACTUAL	DIFFERENCE
TOTAL INCOME			
TOTAL EXPENSES			
TOTAL SAVINGS			

EXPENSE TRACKER

MONTH: ____________________

DATE	DESCRIPTION	CATEGORY	NET AFTER TAX
		TOTAL	

EXPENSE TRACKER

MONTH: ______________________________

DATE	DESCRIPTION	CATEGORY	NET AFTER TAX
		TOTAL	

EXPENSE TRACKER

MONTH: ______________________

DATE	DESCRIPTION	CATEGORY	NET AFTER TAX
		TOTAL	

EXPENSE TRACKER

MONTH: ____________________

DATE	DESCRIPTION	CATEGORY	NET AFTER TAX
		TOTAL	

NOTES

Brain Bump

November

Notes

Priority

1.
2.
3.
4.
5.

Tasks

- [ ]
- [ ]
- [ ]
- [ ]

Don't Forget

MONTHLY BUDGET

MONTH: ______________________ BUDGET GOAL: ____________

YOUR INCOME			
DATE	SOURCE	GROSS AMOUNT	NET AFTER TAX

FIXED EXPENSES		
DATE	DESCRIPTION	AMOUNT
	TOTAL	

VARIABLES EXPENSES		
DATE	DESCRIPTION	AMOUNT
	TOTAL	

	MONTHLY TOTALS		
	BUDGTED	ACTUAL	DIFFERENCE
TOTAL INCOME			
TOTAL EXPENSES			
TOTAL SAVINGS			

EXPENSE TRACKER

MONTH: ______________________________

DATE	DESCRIPTION	CATEGORY	NET AFTER TAX
		TOTAL	

EXPENSE TRACKER

MONTH: ______________________________

DATE	DESCRIPTION	CATEGORY	NET AFTER TAX
		TOTAL	

EXPENSE TRACKER

MONTH: ______________________________

DATE	DESCRIPTION	CATEGORY	NET AFTER TAX
		TOTAL	

EXPENSE TRACKER

MONTH: ______________________________

DATE	DESCRIPTION	CATEGORY	NET AFTER TAX
		TOTAL	

NOTES

Brain Bump

December

Notes

Priority

1.
2.
3.
4.
5.

Tasks

- [ ]
- [ ]
- [ ]
- [ ]

Don't Forget

MONTHLY BUDGET

MONTH: ______________________ BUDGET GOAL: ____________

YOUR INCOME			
DATE	SOURCE	GROSS AMOUNT	NET AFTER TAX

FIXED EXPENSES		
DATE	DESCRIPTION	AMOUNT
	TOTAL	

VARIABLES EXPENSES		
DATE	DESCRIPTION	AMOUNT
	TOTAL	

	MONTHLY TOTALS		
	BUDGTED	ACTUAL	DIFFERENCE
TOTAL INCOME			
TOTAL EXPENSES			
TOTAL SAVINGS			

EXPENSE TRACKER

MONTH: ______________________

DATE	DESCRIPTION	CATEGORY	NET AFTER TAX
		TOTAL	

EXPENSE TRACKER

MONTH: ____________________

DATE	DESCRIPTION	CATEGORY	NET AFTER TAX
		TOTAL	

EXPENSE TRACKER

MONTH: ______________________________

DATE	DESCRIPTION	CATEGORY	NET AFTER TAX
		TOTAL	

EXPENSE TRACKER

MONTH: ______________________________

DATE	DESCRIPTION	CATEGORY	NET AFTER TAX
		TOTAL	

NOTES

Brain Bump

Miscellaneous

Miscellaneous

Made in the USA
Monee, IL
04 November 2026

67385010R00058